Help with HOMEWORK

Key Sta... MATHS

DON'T PANIC SATS

AUTUMN PUBLISHING

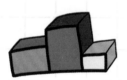

DON'T PANIC
SATS

AUTUMN
PUBLISHING

Published in 2020
by Autumn Publishing
Cottage Farm
Sywell
NN6 0BJ
www.autumnpublishing.co.uk

Copyright © 2019 Autumn Publishing
Autumn is an imprint of Bonnier Books UK

0920 002
2 4 6 8 10 9 7 5 3
ISBN 978-1-83852-671-9

Written by Amy Italiano
Illustrated by Katie Abey

Designed by Chris Stanley
Edited by Suzanne Fossey

Printed and manufactured in China

Key Stage 2 MATHS

An introduction

In Key Stage 2 SATs, you will complete three maths test papers.

Paper 1 is an Arithmetic test, which will contain questions without words that ensure you can use your number skills to calculate. You will have 30 minutes to complete it. The first part of this book (pages 4–17) covers the questions that you will find in the Arithmetic test.

Papers 2 and 3 are Problem Solving and Reasoning tests, where you will have to read questions with words and work out what to do to solve the problems. You will have 40 minutes to complete each of these tests. The second part of this book (pages 18–43) covers areas that you will come across in these two papers.

Parent Guide

Each topic has a guide with tips that you can use to help your child understand and gain confidence in each subject.

Contents

Addition and Subtraction

Adding in Columns

You should be able to add two or more large numbers. They may not be of the same length. Making sure that you line them up carefully with each digit in its correct column will make the calculations a lot easier. If the question uses decimal numbers, line up the decimal points, too!

Try these additions:

①
```
   134
 +  76
-------
   210
```

②
```
  2123
 +  45
-------
  2168
```

③
```
  12356
+ 34567
-------
  46923
```

④
```
  2456
  3485
 + 903
-------
  6844
```

⑤
```
   31.4
 + 23.9
-------
   55.3
```

⑥
```
  31.23
 + 0.87
-------
  32.10
```

⑦
```
  298.70
 + 14.55
--------
  313.25
```

Subtracting in Columns

Set out subtraction questions in the same way as additions, with each digit lined up carefully. You must put the largest number above the smallest number. Don't forget to line up the decimal points!

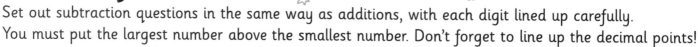

⑧
```
   314
 - 203
-------
   111
```

⑨
```
  5⁵6̷09
 - 4418
-------
  1191
```

⑩
```
  123⁰7̷8
 -   309
--------
  12009
```

⑪
```
   38.9
 - 27.6
-------
   11.3
```

⑫
```
  3498.⁶7̷0
 -   23.65
----------
  3475.05
```

⑬
```
  ⁸9̷.⁹0̷0
 -  3.18
--------
   5.82
```

 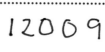

Answers on page 44

Practice Questions

1   4897 + 67 =

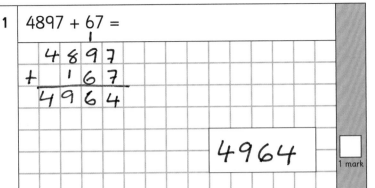

```
    1
  4 8 9 7
+   1 6 7
  4 9 6 4
```

4964

1 mark

2   9.2 + 121 =

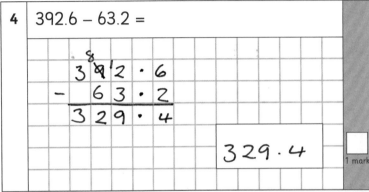

```
    1 9 · 2
+ 1 2 1 · 0
  1 3 0 · 2
```

130·2

1 mark

3   349 − 255 =

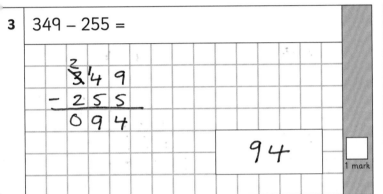

```
    2
  3 4 9
− 2 5 5
  0 9 4
```

94

1 mark

4   392.6 − 63.2 =

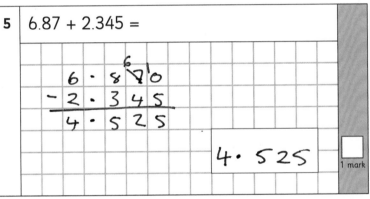

```
      8
  3 9 2 · 6
−   6 3 · 2
  3 2 9 · 4
```

329·4

1 mark

5   6.87 + 2.345 =

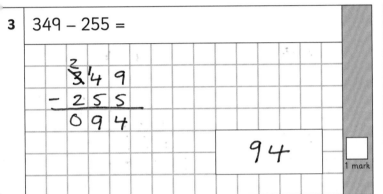

```
          6
  6 · 8 7 0
− 2 · 3 4 5
  4 · 5 2 5
```

4·525

1 mark

6   8452 − 51 =

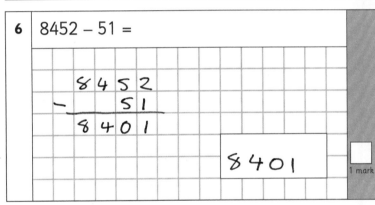

```
  8 4 5 2
−     5 1
  8 4 0 1
```

8401

1 mark

7   9 − 1.9 =

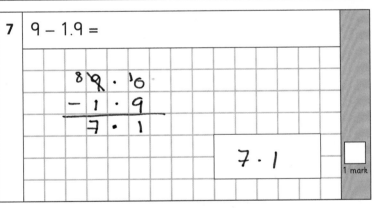

```
  8 8 · 1 0
−   1 · 9
    7 · 1
```

7·1

1 mark

8   27 + 121.8 =

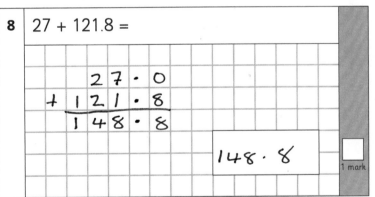

```
    2 7 · 0
+ 1 2 1 · 8
  1 4 8 · 8
```

148·8

1 mark

Multiplication and Division

Short and Long Multiplication

A large number multiplied by a 1-digit number is called short multiplication.

A number multiplied by a 2-digit number is called long multiplication, because you will have to times the big number by the ones digit, *and* the tens digit. Remember to make sure you line up the digits carefully!

Try these:

①
```
    245
  ×   3
 ------
    735
```

②
```
    874
  ×   4
 ------
   3496
```

③
```
    298
  ×  32
 ------
    596
 + 8940
 ------
   9536
```

④
```
    4309
  ×   26
 ------
   25854
 + 86180
 ------
  112034
```

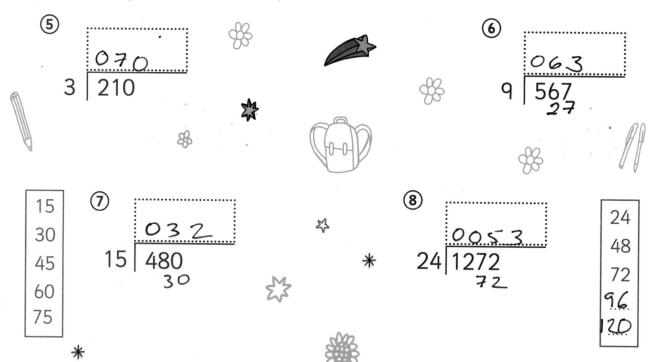

Short and Long Division

When dividing by a 2-digit number, it can be helpful to write out the first multiples in its times table before you start the question.

⑤
```
   070
3 | 210
```

⑥
```
   063
9 | 567
     27
```

⑦
```
    032
15 | 480
      30
```

15
30
45
60
75

⑧
```
    0053
24 | 1272
       72
```

24
48
72
96
120

6

Practice Questions

1 $412 \times 7 =$

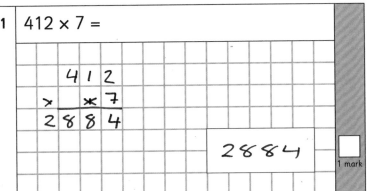

```
    4 1 2
  × * 7
  2 8 8 4
```

2884

1 mark

2 $9813 \times 32 =$

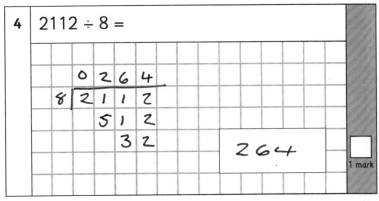

```
      9 8 1 3
    × *   3 2
      1 9 6 2 6
  + 2 9 4 3 9 0
    3 1 4 0 1 6
    * * * *
```

314016

1 mark

3 $219 \times 9 =$

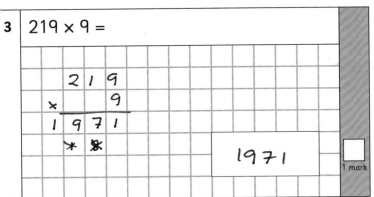

```
    2 1 9
  ×     9
  1 9 7 1
    * *
```

1971

1 mark

4 $2112 \div 8 =$

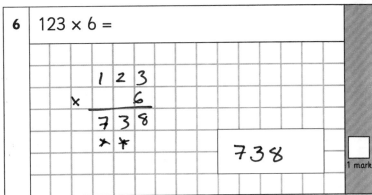

```
      0 2 6 4
  8 ⟌ 2 1 1 2
        5 1 2
          3 2
```

264

1 mark

5 $814 \div 37 =$

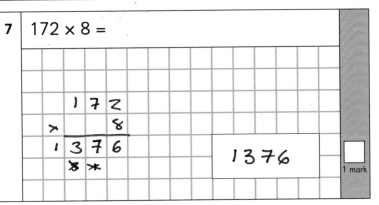

```
37    1×
74    2×
111   3×
```

```
      0 2 2
  3 7 ⟌ 8 1 4
        7 4
```

22

1 mark

6 $123 \times 6 =$

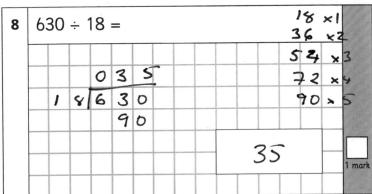

```
    1 2 3
  ×     6
    7 3 8
    * *
```

738

1 mark

7 $172 \times 8 =$

```
    1 7 2
  ×     8
  1 3 7 6
    * *
```

1376

1 mark

8 $630 \div 18 =$

```
18  ×1
36  ×2
54  ×3
72  ×4
90  ×5
```

```
      0 3 5
  1 8 ⟌ 6 3 0
          9 0
```

35

1 mark

Parent Guide

Quick recall of times tables will really help your child to complete these calculations. Look for games or other ways to practise times tables regularly and spontaneously. Resist the urge to use your calculator and work out tough calculations together using pen and paper.

Order of Operations

Sometimes you will see a number sentence with more than one calculation, or operation, in it. It may also contain brackets.

For example:
$$(4 + 6) \div 2 =$$

There is an order to which parts of the number sentence you should work out first. You can remember this order using the word BODMAS:

 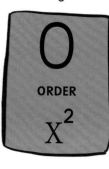    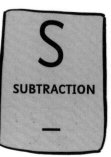

B	O	D	M	A	S
BRACKETS	ORDER	DIVISION	MULTIPLICATION	ADDITION	SUBTRACTION
( )	x^2	$\div$	$\times$	$+$	$-$

In the example question $(4 + 6) \div 2 =$, there are brackets. So, you should work out $4 + 6$ first, which is 10. Then you can do the division:

$$(4 + 6) \div 2 = \longrightarrow 10 \div 2 = 5$$

If there were no brackets and the number sentence looked like this: $4 + 6 \div 2 =$, then BODMAS tells you to do the division before the addition.

$$4 + \boxed{6 \div 2} = \longrightarrow 4 + 3 = 7$$

Use your knowledge of BODMAS to circle around the part in each number sentence that should be calculated first:

① $20 - (4 \times 2) = 12$
    8

② $(15 \div 5) - 3 = 0$
    3

③ $23 - (18 \div 3) = 17$
    6

④ $(3 \times 2) + 6 = 12$
    6

⑤ $17 + (3 \times 6) = 35$
    18

⑥ $(14 \div 2) - (10 \div 5) = 5$
    $7 2$

Parent Guide

Spend time with your child looking at how following the order of operations affects the answer they calculate. Ask questions like "What if the brackets were here? Or here?" and "What if there were no brackets?" This will help them to understand how to apply BODMAS.

Answers on page 44

Practice Questions

1 $45 \div (20 - 5) =$
        ₁₅

$15\overline{)45}$
```
          1 5
          3 0
          4 5
```

3

2 $(35 \div 5) \times 7 =$
         ₇

$7 \times 7 = 49$

49

3 $(9 \times 3) - 4 =$
        ₂₇

$27 - 4 = 23$

23

4 $(5 \times 5) - (3 \times 4) =$
        ₂₅   ₁₂

```
2 5   × 1 2      2 5
                - 1 2
                  1 3
```

13

5 $4 + (7 \times 5) =$
           ₃₅

$4 + 35 = 39$

39

6 $20 - (6 \times 2) =$
            ₁₂

$20 - 12 = 8$

8

7 $12 + (3 \times 2) =$
             ₆

$12 + 6 = 18$

18

8 $50 - (6 \times 6) =$
             ₃₆

$50 - 36 = 14$

14

1 mark

Place Value Calculations

Multiplying by 10, 100 or 1000

When you multiply a number by 10, each digit moves one place value column to the left. The easiest way to do this is to move the decimal point **one** place to the right. When multiplying by 100, move the decimal point **two** places to the right, and to multiply by 1000, move it **three** places to the right.

For example: $31.42 \times 10 = 314.2$ $71.14 \times 100 = 7114$

Try these: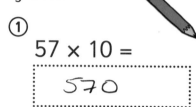

①
$57 \times 10 =$
$$570$$

②
$43.354 \times 100 =$
$$4335.4$$

③
$0.4 \times 1000 =$
$$400$$

Dividing by 10, 100 or 1000

Dividing by 10, 100 or 1000 is just the opposite of multiplying! When you divide by 10, move the decimal point **one** place to the left. When dividing by 100, move it **two** places to the left. When you divide by 1000, move the decimal point **three** places to the left.

For example:

$31.42 \div 10 = 3.142$  $71 \div 100 = 0.71$

Try these:

④
$57 \div 10 =$
$$5.7$$

⑤
$43.3 \div 100 =$
$$0.433$$

⑥
$4 \div 1000 =$
$$0.004$$

REMEMBER!
Multiplying = move the decimal point to the **right**.
Dividing = move the decimal point to the **left**.

Parent Guide

Money is a good way for children to practise these types of calculations without having to write them out in full as they did on pages 6–7.

"How much would it cost for 10 of these?"

"If it costs £3.20 for 10 items, how much is just one item?"

Practice Questions

1 | 76.23 × 10 =

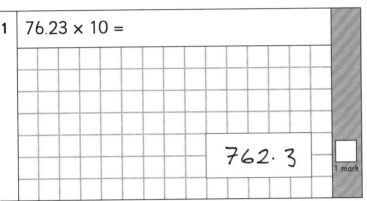

762.3   1 mark

2 | 458 ÷ 1000 =

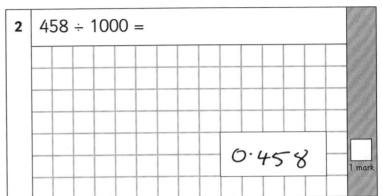

0.458   1 mark

3 | 8.2 ÷ 100 =

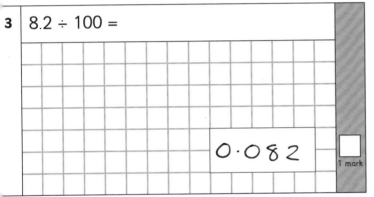

0.082   1 mark

4 | 0.9 ÷ 10 =

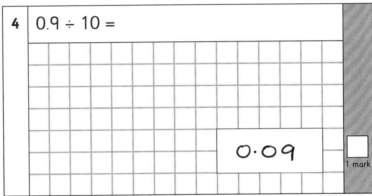

0.09   1 mark

5 | 5.1 × 100 =

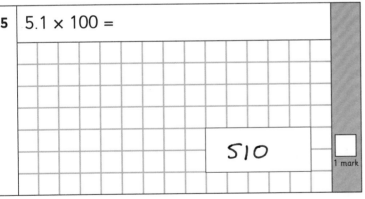

510   1 mark

6 | 62.13 ÷ 100 =

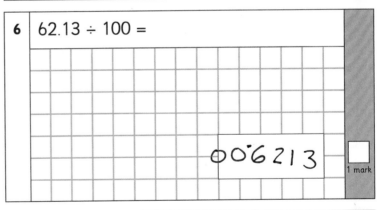

0.6213   1 mark

7 | 62 ÷ 10 =

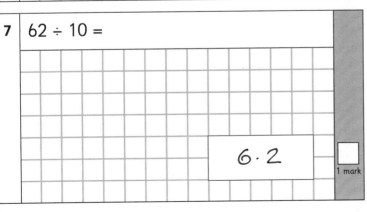

6.2   1 mark

8 | 22.2 × 1000 =

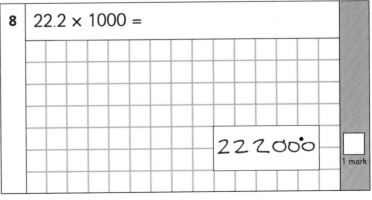

22200.0   1 mark

Percentages

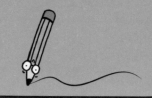

Finding a percentage (%) of a number can be hard but you can make it easier for yourself by finding a simple percentage of the number first.

Find 50% by halving the number.

Find 10% by dividing the number by 10.

Find 5% by halving 10%.

Find 1% by dividing 10% by 10 again.

You might see a percentage question written as "16% of 280" or "16% × 280". "Of" and "×" mean the same thing, so don't panic! You can work out both styles of question in the same way.

For example:

280

$$50\% = 140 \qquad 10\% = 28 \qquad 5\% = 14 \qquad 1\% = 2.8$$

Now you can use the parts you have found to help you with different questions:

$$16\% = 10\% + 5\% + 1\%$$
$$16\% = 28 + 14 + 2.8 = 44.8$$

Try working out these percentages of 280, using the facts above to help you:

①
$$25\% = 10\% + 10\% + 5\%$$
$$25\% = \boxed{} + \boxed{} + \boxed{} = \boxed{}$$

②
$$61\% = 50\% + 10\% + 1\%$$
$$61\% = \boxed{} + \boxed{} + \boxed{} = \boxed{}$$

Parent Guide

Percentages are often a hard concept for children to grasp. Try to talk about them regularly, showing the link to fractions. Calculate together one half (50%), one quarter (25%) or one tenth (10%) of an amount.

Practice Questions

1 20% of 130 =

1 mark

2 25% of 460 =

1 mark

3 50% of 340 =

1 mark

4 51% × 300 =

1 mark

5 30% × 2000 =

1 mark

6 14% of 1600 =

1 mark

7 70% × 190 =

1 mark

8 11% × 567 =

1 mark

Answers on page 44

Adding and Subtracting Fractions

When you are adding or subtracting fractions, it is really important to remember that you can only do the calculation if the fractions have **the same denominator** (the bottom number).

For example:

$$\frac{3}{4} - \frac{1}{4} = \frac{2}{4}$$

⟵ The denominators are all 4.

If you have three quarters of a pizza and somebody takes away one quarter, you will only have two quarters left. Use the **numerators** (the top numbers) to calculate 3 − 1 = 2 and **keep the denominator the same**.

Try these. Make sure to double check whether they are **+** or **−**.

① $\frac{2}{8} + \frac{3}{8} = \boxed{\frac{5}{8}}$

② $\frac{7}{9} - \frac{2}{9} = \boxed{\frac{5}{9}}$

③ $\frac{4}{10} + \frac{5}{10} = \boxed{\frac{9}{10}}$

④ $\frac{5}{6} - \frac{1}{6} = \boxed{\frac{4}{6}}$

If the fractions don't have the same denominator, you will have to convert one or both of them before completing the calculation.

For example: $\frac{1}{4} + \frac{3}{8} =$

If you double the digits in $\frac{1}{4}$ you find an equivalent fraction of $\frac{2}{8}$.
Now you can complete the addition.

$$\times 2 \left(\frac{1}{4} + \frac{3}{8} \right.$$
$$\frac{2}{8} + \frac{3}{8} = \frac{5}{8}$$

Sometimes you will need to convert both fractions to find a common denominator.

$$\frac{4}{5} - \frac{1}{4}$$
$$\times 4 \qquad \times 5$$
$$\frac{16}{20} - \frac{5}{20} = \frac{11}{20}$$

Parent Guide

Children need lots of practical experience with fractions to understand and use the correct vocabulary. Discuss fractions when you are sharing food or other items. Talking about equivalent fractions will help them to understand and find common denominators.

Practice Questions

1 $\dfrac{4}{7} - \dfrac{3}{7} =$

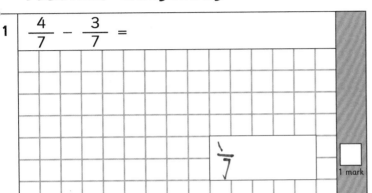

$\dfrac{1}{7}$

1 mark

2 $\dfrac{1}{5} + \dfrac{3}{5} =$

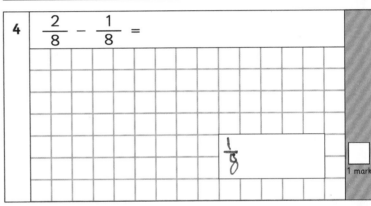

$\dfrac{4}{5}$

1 mark

3 $\dfrac{5}{7} - \dfrac{1}{7} =$

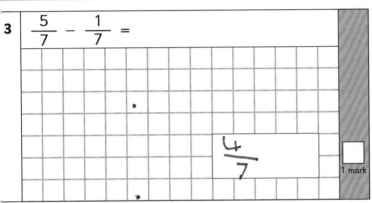

$\dfrac{4}{7}$

1 mark

4 $\dfrac{2}{8} - \dfrac{1}{8} =$

$\dfrac{1}{8}$

1 mark

5 $\dfrac{2}{10} + \dfrac{1}{5} =$

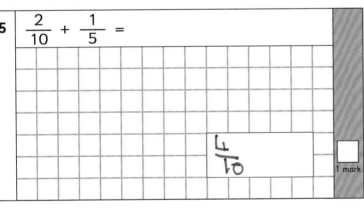

$\dfrac{4}{10}$

1 mark

6 $\dfrac{11}{16} - \dfrac{2}{8} =$

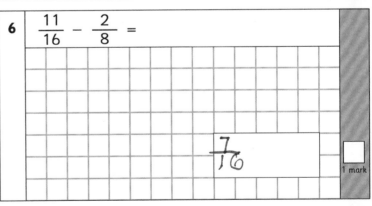

$\dfrac{7}{16}$

1 mark

7 $\dfrac{1}{4} + \dfrac{2}{12} =$

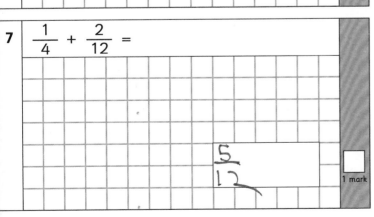

$\dfrac{5}{12}$

1 mark

8 $\dfrac{4}{9} + \dfrac{1}{2} =$

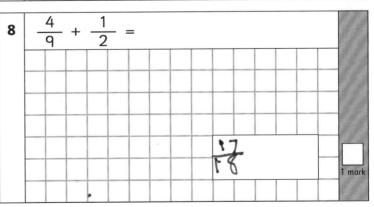

$\dfrac{17}{18}$

1 mark

15

Multiplying and Dividing Fractions

Multiplying Fractions

There are two types of multiplication questions that you might see: multiplying by a whole number and multiplying by another fraction. When multiplying a fraction by a whole number, you **multiply the numerator** and **keep the denominator the same.**

For example:

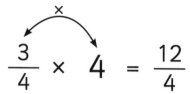

$$\frac{3}{4} \times 4 = \frac{12}{4}$$

When multiplying two fractions, you **multiply the numerators and the denominators**.

For example:

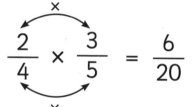

$$\frac{2}{4} \times \frac{3}{5} = \frac{6}{20}$$

Try these:

① $\dfrac{1}{3} \times 2 = \boxed{\dfrac{2}{3}}$

② $\dfrac{3}{4} \times \dfrac{1}{2} = \boxed{\dfrac{3}{8}}$

③ $\dfrac{2}{5} \times 6 = \boxed{\dfrac{12}{5}}$

④ $\dfrac{4}{5} \times \dfrac{2}{3} = \boxed{\dfrac{8}{15}}$

Dividing Fractions

This is the opposite of multiplying. Instead of multiplying the numerator, **multiply the denominator by the whole number.**

For example:

$$\frac{3}{4} \div 2 = \frac{3}{8}$$

Try these:

⑤ $\dfrac{3}{4} \div 5 = \boxed{\dfrac{3}{20}}$

⑥ $\dfrac{1}{3} \div 3 = \boxed{\dfrac{4}{3}}$

⑦ $\dfrac{2}{5} \div 2 = \boxed{\dfrac{2}{10}}$

⑧ $\dfrac{3}{10} \div 4 = \boxed{\dfrac{3}{40}}$

Answers on page 45

Practice Questions

1 $\dfrac{1}{4} \div 3 =$

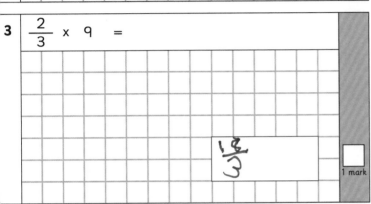

$\dfrac{1}{12}$

1 mark

2 $\dfrac{1}{2} \times 4 =$

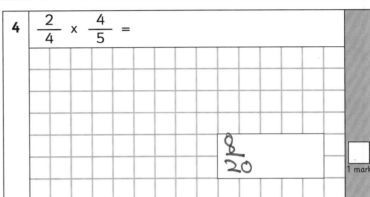

$\dfrac{4}{2}$

1 mark

3 $\dfrac{2}{3} \times 9 =$

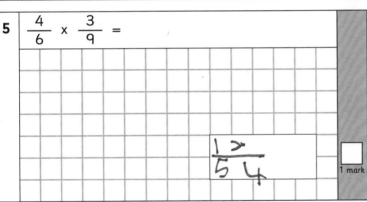

$\dfrac{18}{3}$

1 mark

4 $\dfrac{2}{4} \times \dfrac{4}{5} =$

$\dfrac{8}{20}$

1 mark

5 $\dfrac{4}{6} \times \dfrac{3}{9} =$

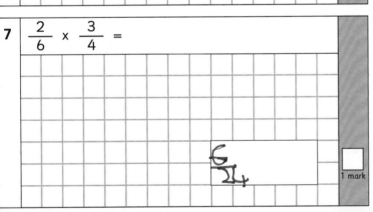

$\dfrac{12}{54}$

1 mark

6 $\dfrac{2}{3} \div 6 =$

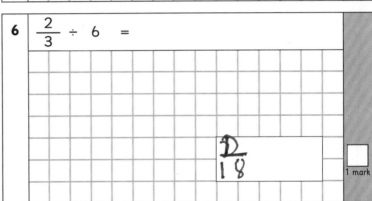

$\dfrac{2}{18}$

1 mark

7 $\dfrac{2}{6} \times \dfrac{3}{4} =$

$\dfrac{6}{24}$

1 mark

8 $\dfrac{5}{7} \div 7 =$

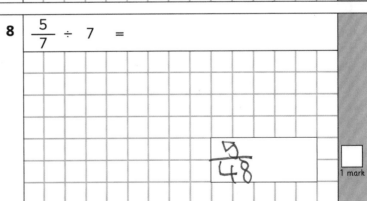

$\dfrac{5}{49}$

1 mark

Parent Guide

Remembering how to apply each operation to fractions can take some time to learn. Try to develop a way of remembering which part will change when multiplying or dividing, such as:

Times = **t**op

Divide = **d**enominator

Encourage your child to join these parts with arrows as shown in the examples.

Place Value

Sometimes you may come across some really big numbers. Don't panic! You can use commas to break them up and see each digit's place value.

For example:

3 2 , 4 5 6 , 1 0 2

Ten Millions
Millions
Hundred Thousands
Ten Thousands
Thousands
Hundreds
Tens
Ones

① Write this number in words:

② In this number, the value of the digit "5" is 50,000. What is the value of the digit "1"?

③ What is the value of the digit "4"?

④ In this number, the digit "2" is in the millions column. Which digit is in the ones column?

⑤ Which digit is in the ten millions column?

⑦ What is one hundred less than this number?

⑥ What is one more than this number?

Decimal Place Value

It is also important to learn the place value of decimal numbers so that you can order and convert them into fractions and percentages. These are the decimal place value parts you need to know:

0.2 3 6

Tenths
Hundredths
Thousandths

⑧ What is one tenth more than this number?

⑨ What is one hundredth less than this number?

⑩ Which digit is in the thousandths column?

18

Practice Questions

① Order these from **biggest** to **smallest**.

£3,123,000   £1,500,000

£280,000   £518,750

<table>
<tr><td></td></tr>
<tr><td></td></tr>
<tr><td></td></tr>
<tr><td></td></tr>
</table>

1 mark

② Write the **largest** number from question 1 in words.

_____

_____

_____

1 mark

③ Order these from **shortest** to **longest**.

1.24m   0.24m   10.4m   1.23m

<table>
<tr><td></td></tr>
<tr><td></td></tr>
<tr><td></td></tr>
<tr><td></td></tr>
</table>

1 mark

④ Start with 3,942,309 and add the following to the original number.

1 more: [ ]

1,000 more: [ ]

100,000 more: [ ]

1 mark

⑤   0.752

Which digit is in the tenths column?

[ ]

1 mark

⑥ What is one thousandth less than 0.752?

[ ]

1 mark

Negative Numbers

Negative numbers are numbers below 0. Using a number line is a really good way of understanding negative numbers. It will help you to add or subtract using negative numbers, or find a difference that crosses zero on a number line.

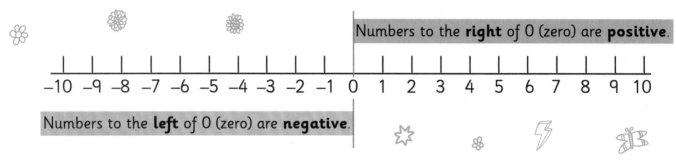

Numbers to the **right** of 0 (zero) are **positive**.

-10 -9 -8 -7 -6 -5 -4 -3 -2 -1 0 1 2 3 4 5 6 7 8 9 10

Numbers to the **left** of 0 (zero) are **negative**.

Adding or Subtracting

If you **add** a number, jump to the **right**. If you **subtract** a number, jump to the **left**.

For example: $4 - 9 =$

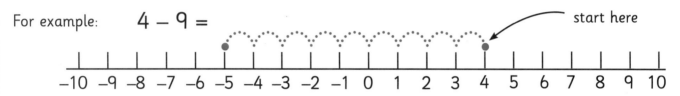

start here

-10 -9 -8 -7 -6 -5 -4 -3 -2 -1 0 1 2 3 4 5 6 7 8 9 10

Start at 4, make 9 jumps to the left and you land on -5.

Try these, using the number line at the top of the page to help:

① $3 - 6 =$

② $-3 + 6 =$

③ $-1 - 3 =$

④ $-8 + 2 =$

Finding a Difference

You may also be given two numbers and asked to find the difference between them. Mark the two numbers on a number line and count the jumps between them.

For example: Difference between -3 and $6 =$

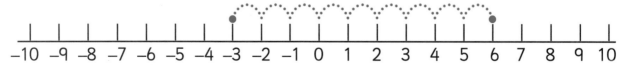

-10 -9 -8 -7 -6 -5 -4 -3 -2 -1 0 1 2 3 4 5 6 7 8 9 10

There are nine jumps between -3 and 6 so the difference between the two numbers is 9.

Try these:

⑤ Difference between
   -4 and $6 =$

⑥ Difference between
   -2 and $4 =$

⑦ Difference between
   -10 and $-4 =$

Answers on page 45

Practice Questions

① Fill in the positive and negative numbers on the number line.

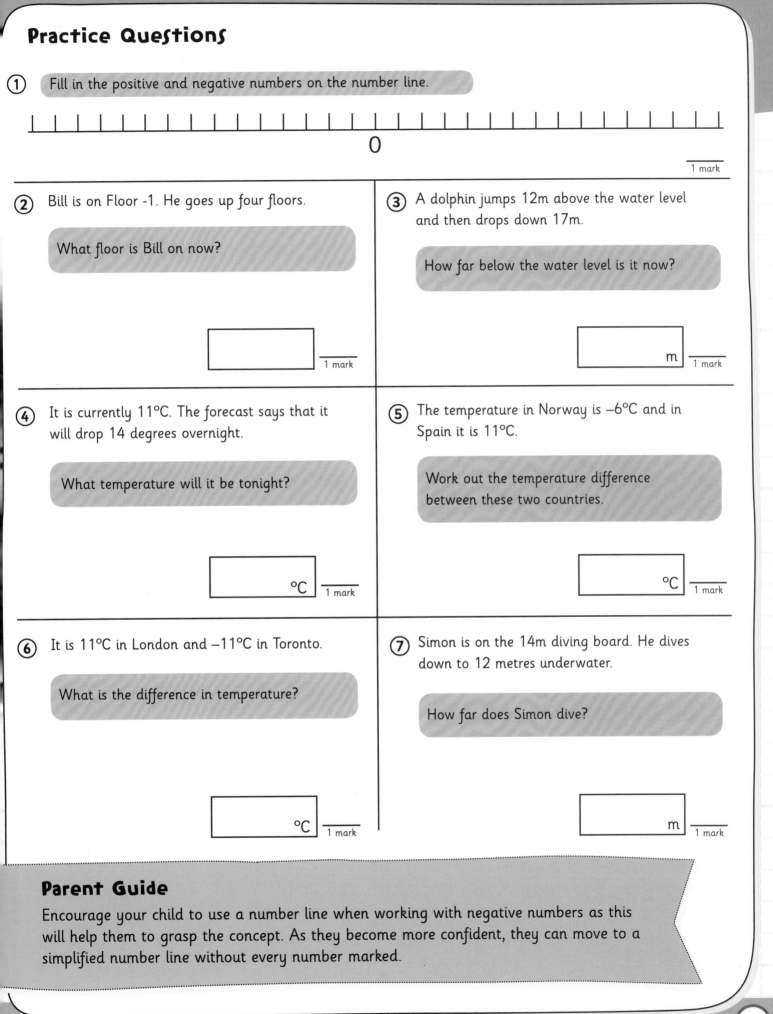

0

1 mark

② Bill is on Floor -1. He goes up four floors.

What floor is Bill on now?

1 mark

③ A dolphin jumps 12m above the water level and then drops down 17m.

How far below the water level is it now?

m   1 mark

④ It is currently 11°C. The forecast says that it will drop 14 degrees overnight.

What temperature will it be tonight?

°C   1 mark

⑤ The temperature in Norway is −6°C and in Spain it is 11°C.

Work out the temperature difference between these two countries.

°C   1 mark

⑥ It is 11°C in London and −11°C in Toronto.

What is the difference in temperature?

°C   1 mark

⑦ Simon is on the 14m diving board. He dives down to 12 metres underwater.

How far does Simon dive?

m   1 mark

Parent Guide
Encourage your child to use a number line when working with negative numbers as this will help them to grasp the concept. As they become more confident, they can move to a simplified number line without every number marked.

Rounding

Rounding is an important skill which tests your knowledge of place value and helps with estimating. You will need to remember your place value columns and visualise the numbers on a number line.

For example: **Round 2,340 to the nearest 1,000**

- Find the 1,000s column: **2**,340
- This number would be between 2,000 and 3,000 on a number line. Which one would it be closer to? Look at the digit to the right: 2,**3**40
- If the digit to the right is **four or less, round down.** If the digit to the right is **five or more, round up.** As it is a three, it means that the number is closer to 2,000.

The answer is 2,000

Try these:

① Round 4,561 to the nearest 1,000.

② Round 32,364 to the nearest 1,000.

③ Round 7,769 to the nearest 100.

④ Round 345,687 to the nearest 100,000.

⑤ Round 459 to the nearest 10.

Estimating

It is important to use rounding to estimate the answers to more difficult calculations. This will ensure your answer is close to the number you were expecting. Estimating like this helps when you don't have a pen and paper or calculator, and you need to work out a rough answer in your head quickly.

For example: **292 x 6**

292 is very close to 300, so you would do 300 x 6 = 1,800. When you work out 292 x 6, you know that you are expecting an answer that is close to 1,800.

Round these 2-digit numbers to the nearest 10 to work out an estimate:

⑥ 67 x 4 becomes 70 x 4 =

⑦ 81 x 5 becomes __ x 5 =

⑧ 43 x 6 becomes __ x 6 =

⑨ 58 x 3 becomes __ x 3 =

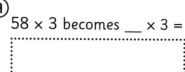

Answers on page 45

Practice Questions

① Round 32,617 to the nearest:

1,000: [ ]

100: [ ]

10,000: [ ]

10: [ ]

1 mark

② Jane is buying 12 packs of pencils that cost £2.99 each.

Work out her estimated spend by rounding the price of one pack to the nearest £1.

£ [ ]

1 mark

③ Ben has to work out an estimate for 42 x 3.2.

Which calculation should he use?

40 x 4   45 x 4   40 x 3   50 x 3

[ ]

1 mark

④ At the cinema you buy a drink costing £1.06 and popcorn that costs £2.90.

Estimate how much money you will need by rounding to the nearest £1.

£ [ ]

1 mark

⑤ Round 452,719 to the nearest:

1,000: [ ]

100: [ ]

10,000: [ ]

100,000: [ ]

1 mark

⑥ Chris needs two pieces of string. One should be 1.92m and the other 2.97m.

Estimate how much string Chris will need by rounding to the nearest metre.

[ ]

1 mark

Parent Guide
Use opportunities like shopping with your child to round prices and calculate rough estimates. Talk about the most effective ways to round numbers in order to create calculations that are accurate but easy to work out mentally.

Answers on page 45

Comparing Fractions

Mixed Numbers and Improper Fractions

Mixed numbers are made up of a whole number and a fraction: $2\frac{3}{4}$

Improper fractions have a larger numerator than the denominator: $\frac{11}{4}$

For example:

In the picture, there are $2\frac{3}{4}$ pizzas. Two of the pizzas are cut into four slices (2 x 4 = 8 quarters) and the last one only has three slices left (8 + 3 = 11). So altogether there are: $\frac{11}{4}$.

Convert these mixed numbers into improper fractions:

① $1\frac{1}{4} = \frac{\boxed{}}{4}$

② $2\frac{2}{3} = \frac{\boxed{}}{3}$

③ $3\frac{1}{2} = \frac{\boxed{}}{2}$

Comparing Fractions

You may be asked to compare two or more fractions and say which is bigger or smaller. To do this, they must have a **common denominator** (that is the number on the bottom of both fractions). You may also be asked to compare mixed numbers. To do this, convert them into improper fractions.

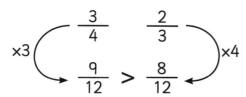

×3 $\left(\dfrac{3}{4} \quad \dfrac{2}{3} \right)$ ×4

$\dfrac{9}{12} > \dfrac{8}{12}$

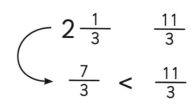

$2\frac{1}{3} \qquad \frac{11}{3}$

$\frac{7}{3} < \frac{11}{3}$

Finding a common denominator shows that $\frac{3}{4}$ is the largest fraction.

Converting to an improper fraction shows that $\frac{11}{3}$ is the largest fraction.

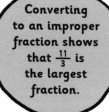

Answers on page 46

Practice Questions

① Put <, > or = between these fractions.

$\frac{2}{3}$ ☐ $\frac{3}{5}$

$\frac{2}{8}$ ☐ $\frac{1}{4}$

$\frac{2}{9}$ ☐ $\frac{1}{3}$

$\frac{3}{10}$ ☐ $\frac{1}{5}$

1 mark

② Natasha eats $\frac{3}{8}$ of her cheese pizza and Leigh eats $\frac{7}{16}$ of her meat feast pizza.

Work out who has eaten the most pizza.

1 mark

③ Ravi has 22 quarters of quiche.

How many whole quiches can Ravi make?

Write your answer as a mixed number.

☐ quiches   1 mark

④ Matthew cuts an apple into five pieces and eats two. Grace cuts hers into 12 pieces and eats five of them.

Who has eaten more of their apple?

1 mark

⑤ Match each mixed number to its improper fraction.

$2\frac{1}{4}$ $\frac{11}{2}$

$5\frac{1}{2}$ $\frac{15}{4}$

$3\frac{3}{4}$ $\frac{9}{4}$

1 mark

⑥ Complete the two boxes to make three equivalent fractions.

$\frac{\boxed{}}{4}$ = $\frac{8}{16}$ = $\frac{4}{\boxed{}}$

1 mark

Fractions, Decimals and Percentages

It is really important to understand the relationship between fractions, decimals and percentages. The best way to see this is by using hundredths, because **percent** means **out of 100**:

$$\frac{5}{100} = 0.05 = 5\%$$

5 hundredths   5 is in the hundredths column   5 out of 100

If you are asked to compare a fraction, decimal or percentage, you can convert them into hundredths so that they are easier to compare.

For example:

$$0.38 \quad\quad 44\% \quad\quad \frac{14}{25}$$

$$\frac{38}{100} \quad\quad \frac{44}{100} \quad\quad \frac{56}{100} \Big) \times 4$$

0.38 is the smallest amount (38 hundredths), 44% is the middle amount (44 hundredths) and $\frac{14}{25}$ is the largest amount (56 hundredths).

Turn these amounts into hundredths:

① $\frac{13}{50}$ → $\dfrac{\boxed{}}{100}$

② 28% → $\dfrac{\boxed{}}{100}$

③ 0.14 → $\dfrac{\boxed{}}{100}$

④ $\frac{2}{10}$ → $\dfrac{\boxed{}}{100}$

  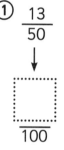 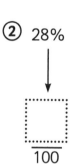 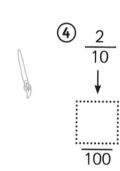 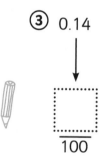

⑤ 0.02 → $\dfrac{\boxed{}}{100}$

⑥ 3% → $\dfrac{\boxed{}}{100}$

⑦ 0.3 → $\dfrac{\boxed{}}{100}$

⑧ 32% → $\dfrac{\boxed{}}{100}$

⑨ $\frac{5}{20}$ → $\dfrac{\boxed{}}{100}$

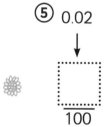 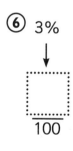 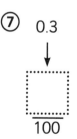 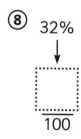 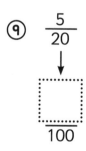

Parent Guide

Your child may find it confusing when given two amounts in different formats. Encourage them to convert the amounts into the same format – whichever one they are most comfortable with. It is an important step when they can see the meaning of decimal place value columns: "two tenths" can mean "2 in the tenths column" (0.2) or $\frac{2}{10}$.

Answers on page 46

Practice Questions

① Sinead scores 54% on her maths test and Ryan completes $\frac{26}{50}$ questions correctly.

Who got the best score?

1 mark

② Tom has a jar of 25 marbles. 13 are striped. That means that 13% of them are striped.

Is this right?

1 mark

③ Put these amounts in order from **smallest** to **largest**:

5%   0.55 $\frac{5}{10}$

1 mark

④ A shopkeeper has a ribbon measuring 100cm. He sells 38cm of it to a customer.

What percentage does he have left?

1 mark

⑤ Harry is in a 25km race and has run 6km. Ian is in a 20km race and has swum 7km.

Who has completed most of their race?

1 mark

⑥ Chin spends 40% of his time practising his goalkeeping and $\frac{3}{5}$ of his time studying.

What does he do the most?

1 mark

Ratio and Proportion

Ratio and proportion are used when something is split into different parts. In this picture, there are several pears and oranges.

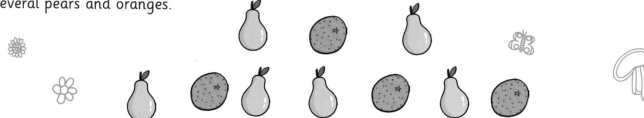

Ratio compares the two parts: there are 4 oranges for every 6 pears. This is a ratio of **4:6**.

Proportion compares a part to the whole amount: there are 10 fruits and four of them are oranges. This is a proportion of **4 in every 10** or $\frac{4}{10}$.

Calculating Ratio

You may be given a ratio and need to work out how many times it has been used.

For example: Dan was tiling his bathroom and used 4 white tiles for every 6 blue tiles. If he used 24 white tiles, how many blue tiles did he use?

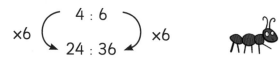

×6 $\left(\begin{array}{c} 4:6 \\ 24:36 \end{array}\right)$ ×6

The ratio is 4:6. He used 24 white tiles – this is 6 lots of the ratio.
So we multiply both sides by 6. This means that he used 36 blue tiles in total.

Work out how many lots of the ratio are being used in the following questions and complete the missing numbers:

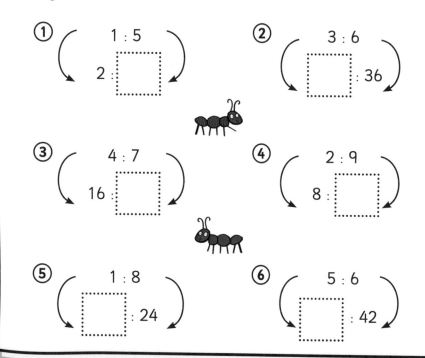

① $\left(\begin{array}{c} 1:5 \\ 2:\boxed{} \end{array}\right)$

② $\left(\begin{array}{c} 3:6 \\ \boxed{}:36 \end{array}\right)$

③ $\left(\begin{array}{c} 4:7 \\ 16:\boxed{} \end{array}\right)$

④ $\left(\begin{array}{c} 2:9 \\ 8:\boxed{} \end{array}\right)$

⑤ $\left(\begin{array}{c} 1:8 \\ \boxed{}:24 \end{array}\right)$

⑥ $\left(\begin{array}{c} 5:6 \\ \boxed{}:42 \end{array}\right)$

Answers on page 46

Practice Questions

1 Sam has three grey, four black and two white rabbits.

Write a fraction to show the proportion of black rabbits.

[   ]
1 mark

2 Now write a ratio to compare grey rabbits to white rabbits.

[   ]
1 mark

3 Sally is making a collage. She uses four shells for every five stones that are included.

Write this as a ratio.

[   ]
1 mark

4 If Sally's picture used 16 shells, how many stones are used?

[   ]
1 mark

5 Sally's sister uses the same ratio to make her own collage. She uses 30 stones.

How many shells will she need?

[   ]
1 mark

6 For every six chocolates you eat, your friends eat eight sweets.

If you ate 12 chocolates, how many sweets did your friends eat?

[   ]
1 mark

Answers on page 46

Units of Measurement

There are lots of facts and figures to remember when measuring. There's time, length, capacity and mass. Here are some key facts you should know:

Length
1 cm = 10 mm
1 metre = 100 cm
1 km = 1000 m

Time
1 minute = 60 seconds
1 hour = 60 minutes
1 day = 24 hours
1 week = 7 days
1 year = 12 months

Mass
1000 milligrams = 1 gram
1 kilogram = 1000 grams

Capacity
1 litre = 1000 millilitres

Parent Guide

Lots of practical activities such as weighing ingredients, pouring drinks and measuring items will help your child to become familiar with units of measurement Look out for rhymes or other ways to remember trickier facts, such as how many days in each month and how many days in a normal year or leap year.

Converting Between Units

You will need to convert between these units of measurement. It is helpful to write down the key fact to help you see whether you need to multiply or divide.

For example:

How many grams in 5.3 kilograms?

The key fact is: **1 kg = 1000g.**

To move from kilograms to grams, the number of kg is multiplied by 1000.

So: 5.3 x 1000 = 5300g.

This is a place value calculation!

How many metres in 348 cm?

The key fact is: **1 metre = 100cm.**

To move from centimetres to metres, the number of cm is divided by 100.

So: 348 ÷ 100 = 3.48m.

Now try these using the key facts from the boxes above to help:

① 360 seconds = ☐ minutes

② 3.1 litres = ☐ millilitres

③ 7 weeks = ☐ days

④ 4200m = ☐ kilometres

⑤ 19 minutes = ☐ seconds

⑥ 48 hours = ☐ days

⑦ 3 years = ☐ months

⑧ 2 kilometres = ☐ metres

30

Practice Questions

① Sarah wants to read 10 pages from her book **every day for three weeks**.

> How many pages will she read altogether in this time?

[ ] 1 mark

② A waitress has a **three litre** jug. She pours two glasses of water which each hold 300ml.

> How many **millilitres** are left in the jug?

[ ] 1 mark

③ A new-born baby is awake for 480 **minutes** each day.

> How many **hours** is he asleep?

[ ] 1 mark

④ Jenny runs 2.8km and John runs 800m.

> How many **kilometres** have they run altogether?

[ ] 1 mark

⑤ Complete this table.

Millimetres	Centimetres	Metres
150		
	200	
		5

1 mark

⑥ My brother is 24 **months** old.

> How many **years** old is he?

[ ] 1 mark

2D Shapes

Parts of 2D Shapes

A 2D shape has 2 parts: sides and vertices. A **side** is the edge of the shape. It can be straight or curved. A **vertex** (plural: vertices) is the corner, or point, where the sides meet.

For example:

A square has:
- 4 sides
- 4 vertices

Try these:

① Trapezium: [　　] sides and [　　] vertices.

② Triangle: [　　] sides and [　　] vertices.

Regular and Irregular

A **regular** shape has sides which are all the **same length** and angles inside each vertex which are **equal**. An **irregular** shape has some **sides and angles** that are **not equal.**

Work out whether these shapes are regular or irregular:

③ [　　　　　]   ④ [　　　　　]   ⑤ [　　　　　]   ⑥ [　　　　　]

Parallel and Perpendicular

A pair of **parallel** sides are exactly the same distance from one another at all times, and point in exactly the same direction. If you continued to draw them, they would never meet. A pair of **perpendicular** sides meet at a right angle (90°).

parallel   perpendicular

Parent Guide

Children often learn to name shapes from a young age, but describing their properties is a greater challenge. Play a game where you make a statement like: "A quadrilateral is a regular shape" and they can decide if the statement is "always true", "sometimes true" or "never true". This will develop their reasoning skills.

Answers on page 47

Practice Questions

(1) Draw a triangle that has a right angle and two equal sides.

Use a ruler.

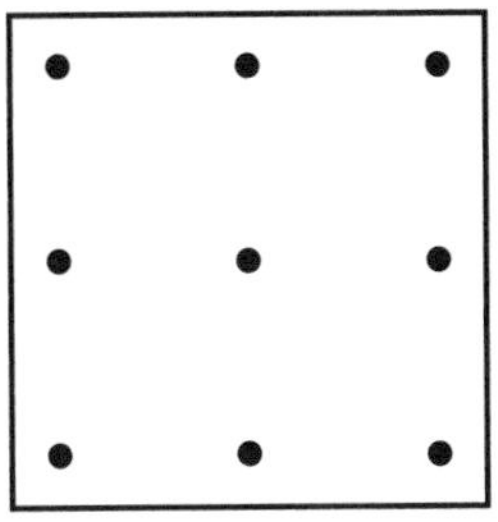

[grid of 9 dots]

(2) Draw a triangle that has two equal sides but **no right angles**.

Use a ruler.

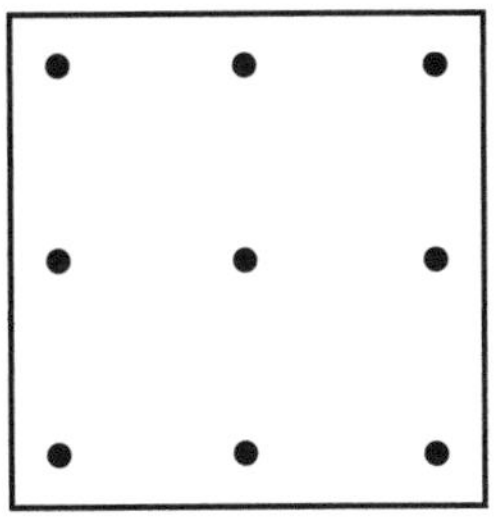

[grid of 9 dots]

1 mark

(3) Draw a parallelogram.

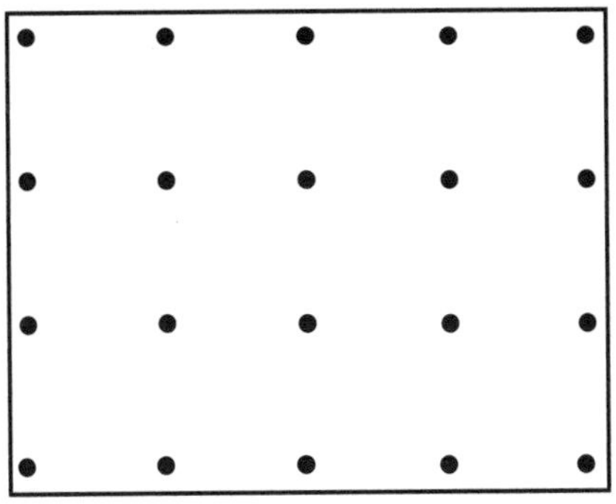

[grid of 20 dots]

1 mark

(4) A circle has a diameter of 10cm.

What is the radius of the circle?

[answer box]

1 mark

(5) Work out which statement belongs to which shape and write the number in the box.

[shape 1]

A. It has 2 pairs of parallel sides.

[box]

[shape 3]

B. It is an irregular pentagon.

[box]

C. It is an isosceles triangle.

[box]

[shape 2]

D. It has 2 pairs of perpendicular sides.

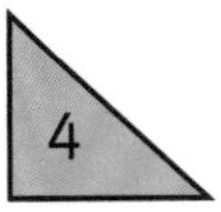

[box]

[shape 4]

1 mark

(6) Write the letters of the two shapes which are pentagons.

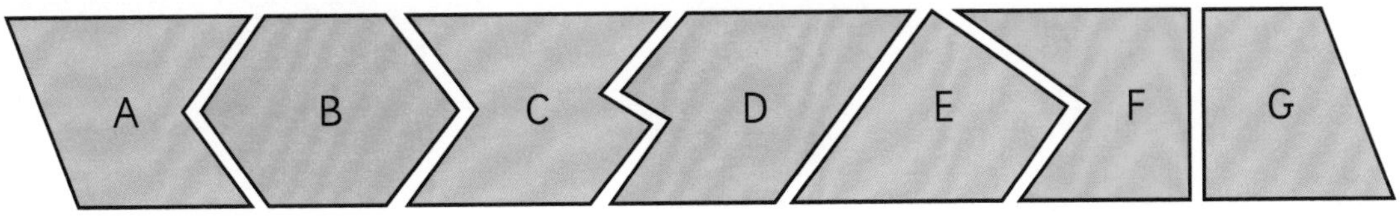

[shapes A B C D E F G]

[box] and [box]

1 mark

33

3D Shapes

Parts of 3D shapes

A 3D shape has 3 parts: faces, edges and vertices. A **face** is the flat surface of a 3D shape. An **edge** is the line where the faces meet and a **vertex** is the corner, or point, where the edges meet.

For example:

A cube has:
- 6 square faces
- 12 edges
- 8 vertices

Try these:

① Triangular prism: ⬚ faces, ⬚ edges and ⬚ vertices.

② Cylinder: ⬚ faces, ⬚ edges and ⬚ vertices.

③ Square-based pyramid: ⬚ faces, ⬚ edges and ⬚ vertices.

④ Cuboid: ⬚ faces, ⬚ edges and ⬚ vertices.

Nets

A net of a 3D shape is what the shape would look like if it was opened up and laid flat. You can fold nets back up to build 3D shapes.

Write the name of the 3D shapes these nets would create if they were folded up:

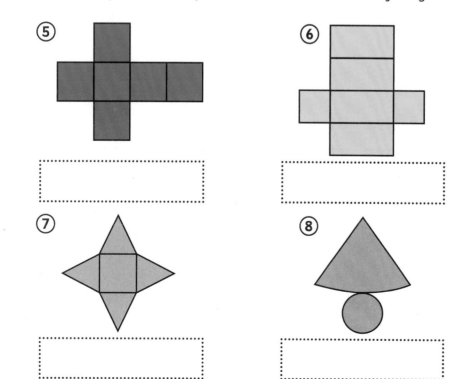

⑤

⑥

⑦

⑧

Parent Guide

Children benefit from practical experience with 3D shapes, like folding nets and model building. These hands-on activities provide a reference point for the visualisation that is required to work with drawn 3D shapes. Encourage them to imagine picking the shape up, turning or folding it.

34

Practice Questions

① Complete the table to describe this shape.

Number of faces	Number of edges	Number of vertices

1 mark

② Draw a dot on the net so that the shape will have dots on opposite faces when it is folded up.

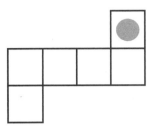

1 mark

③ Draw two more faces to complete this net.

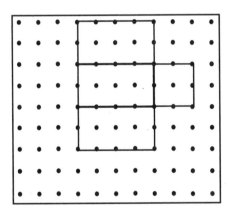

1 mark

④ How many vertices does this shape have?

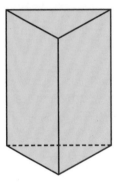

1 mark

⑤ How many faces of this cube are hidden?

1 mark

⑥ Gemma joins four straws to make a square. Then she joins more straws to make a cube.

How many straws has Gemma used?

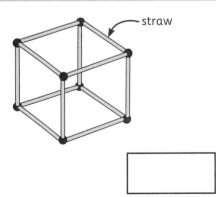

straw

1 mark

Answers on page 47

Perimeter, Area and Volume

Perimeter

Perimeter is the **distance around a shape**. This is calculated by adding all the side lengths together. Work out any sides which aren't labelled before you start adding.

For example:

3cm

2cm   2cm

3cm

① $2 + 3 + 2 + 3 =$ ....

The perimeter of this shape is .... cm.

Area

Area is the size of the inside of a shape and it is measured in square units. If the squares are marked inside a shape, you can count them.

For example:

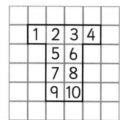

1	2	3	4
	5	6	
	7	8	
	9	10	

Area = 10 square units

If there are no squares marked but the shape is a square or rectangle, you can use the formula **length x width** to work out the area.

For example:

9cm

4cm

② $9 \times 4 =$ ....

The perimeter of this shape is .... cm².

Volume

Volume is the amount of 3D space inside a shape and it is measured in cubic units. If cubes are drawn inside the shape, you can count them to make it easier.

For example:

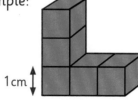

1cm

This shape is built using five 1cm cubes.

Volume = 5 cm³

If there are no cubes marked, but the shape is a cube or a cuboid, you can use the formula **length x width x height** to work out the volume.

For example:

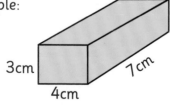

3cm   4cm   7cm

③ $3 \times 4 \times 7 =$ ....

The volume of this shape is .... cm³.

Answers on page 47

Practice Questions

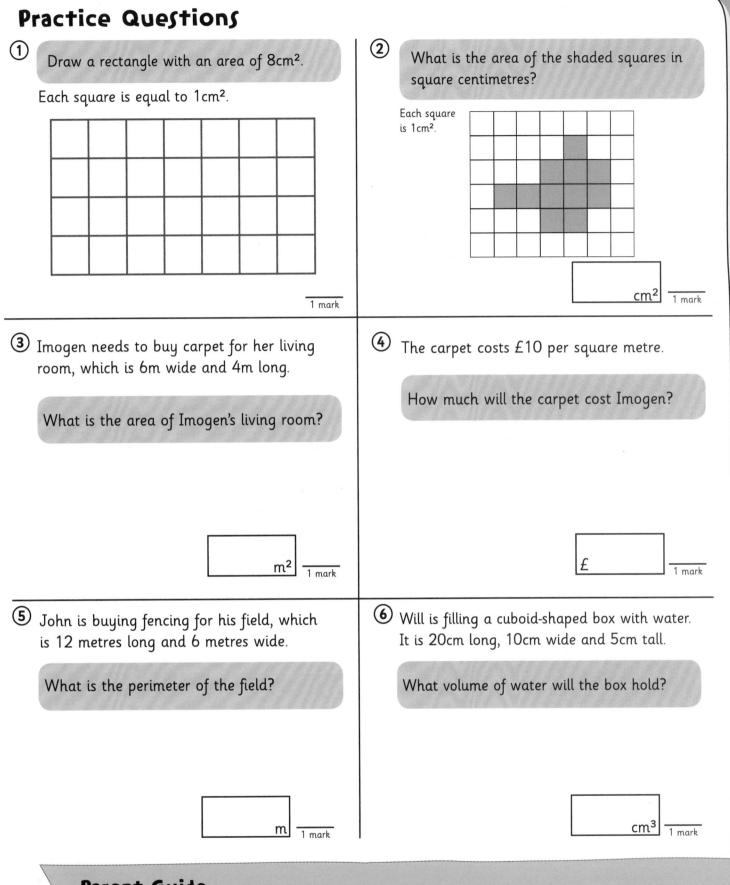

(1) Draw a rectangle with an area of 8cm².

Each square is equal to 1cm².

1 mark

(2) What is the area of the shaded squares in square centimetres?

Each square is 1cm².

cm² 1 mark

(3) Imogen needs to buy carpet for her living room, which is 6m wide and 4m long.

What is the area of Imogen's living room?

m² 1 mark

(4) The carpet costs £10 per square metre.

How much will the carpet cost Imogen?

£ 1 mark

(5) John is buying fencing for his field, which is 12 metres long and 6 metres wide.

What is the perimeter of the field?

m 1 mark

(6) Will is filling a cuboid-shaped box with water. It is 20cm long, 10cm wide and 5cm tall.

What volume of water will the box hold?

cm³ 1 mark

Parent Guide
Children often confuse perimeter and area, and whether they should add or multiply the side lengths. Try to develop a story such as "Peri the Parrot flies around the outside of a shape" or an alliterative reminder such as "Perimeter means Plus" to help.

Angles

An angle is the measurement of a turn between two lines and is measured in degrees. A protractor measures angles, but you can often work out a missing angle using facts you have learnt.

Types of Angle

There are 6 types of angle: **acute, right, straight, obtuse, reflex** and **full angle**.

Write the name of these angles:

① ....

② ....

③ ....

Here are two amazing angle facts that you should learn:

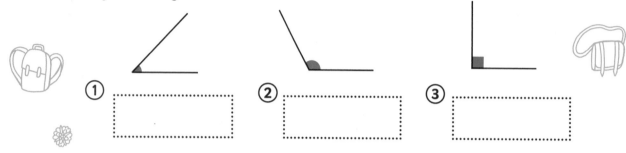

The three angles in a triangle **ALWAYS** add up to **180°**.

The four angles in a quadrilateral **ALWAYS** add up to **360°**.

Using these angle facts, can you work out the missing angles in these shapes?

④ a 70° 50°

70 + 50 = ...

180 − .... = ...

⑤ 52° y

.... + ... = ...

180 − .... = ...

⑥ 80° 75° 105° x

80 + 75 + 105 = ...

360 − .... = ...

Opposite Angles

When two lines cross, the opposite angles are always equal.

For example:

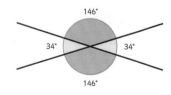

146°
34°   34°
146°

The two smaller opposite angles are both 34°.

The two larger opposite angles are both 146°.

Answers on page 47

Practice Questions

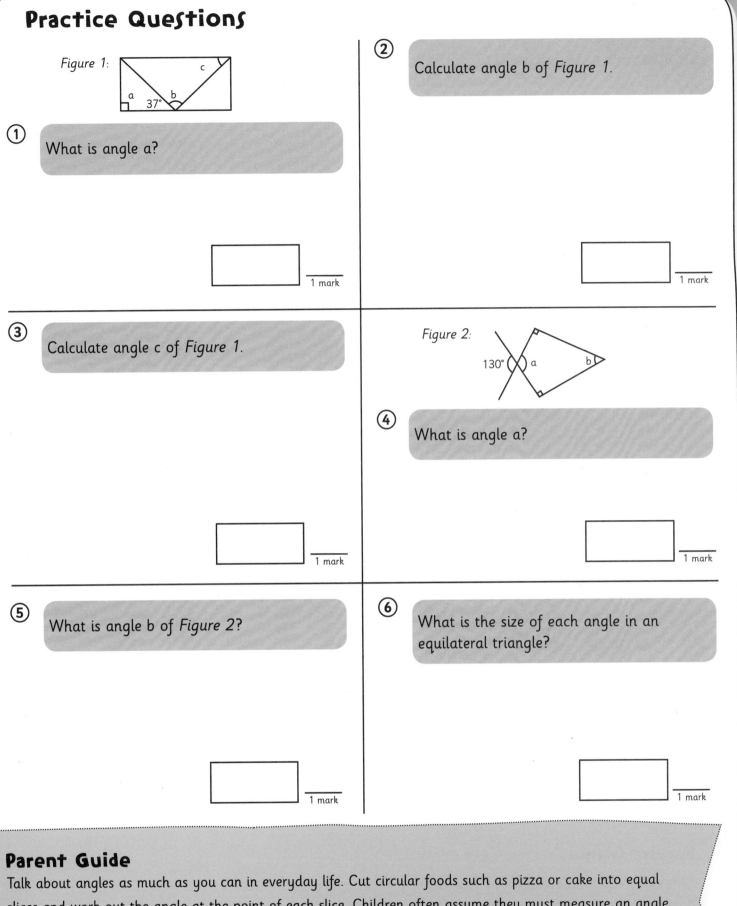

Figure 1:

① What is angle a?

[   ] 1 mark

② Calculate angle b of *Figure 1*.

[   ] 1 mark

③ Calculate angle c of *Figure 1*.

[   ] 1 mark

Figure 2:

④ What is angle a?

[   ] 1 mark

⑤ What is angle b of *Figure 2*?

[   ] 1 mark

⑥ What is the size of each angle in an equilateral triangle?

[   ] 1 mark

Parent Guide
Talk about angles as much as you can in everyday life. Cut circular foods such as pizza or cake into equal slices and work out the angle at the point of each slice. Children often assume they must measure an angle with a protractor to find out how big it is, but if the diagram is not to scale they will have to think about which angle fact to use to work it out!

Coordinates

Coordinates are used to describe a point's position on a grid. These grids will be made of four quadrants (or quarters) with positive and negative numbers, like the number lines you used earlier.

A coordinate is created using two numbers that are separated by a comma and enclosed in brackets, like this: (3,4). The first number tells you how many moves **left or right** from the 0, and the second number tells you how many moves **up or down**.

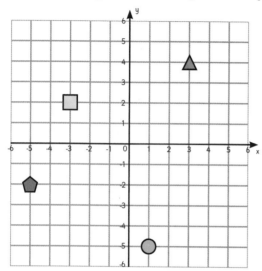

The red triangle has been marked at (3,4). Can you write the coordinates of the other shapes?

① ▢ = (,)

② ⬠ = (,)

③ ⬤ = (,)

Add these shapes to the grid using the coordinates given:

④ ⬡ = (4,1)   ⑤ = (5,–3)   ⑥ ◆ = (–2,–2)

Translation

Translation is when you move a shape on a coordinate grid. You put your finger, or pencil, on one vertex of the shape and follow the translation instructions. Then draw the shape in its new place.

For example:

This shape has been moved **four squares to the right and two squares up.**

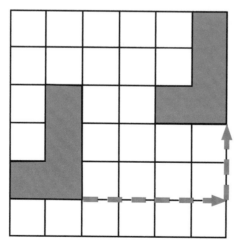

⑦ Move this shape **two squares to the right and four squares up.** Draw it in the new location.

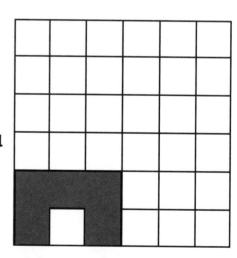

Parent Guide

Children frequently confuse the order of the numbers in a coordinate. Expressions such as "walk before you can fly" or "along the corridor and up the stairs" can help to remind them that the first number is across and the second is up or down. Encourage them to ALWAYS return to the origin (0,0) before plotting or reading a new coordinate.

Answers on page 48

Practice Questions

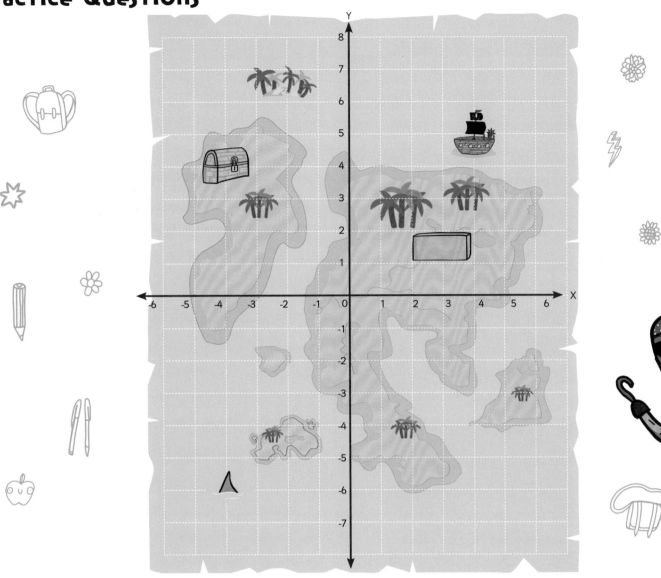

① Mark an 'X' at points (2,–3), (1,–6) and (3,–6).

1 mark

② Join up your marks. What shape have you made?

1 mark

③ Write the coordinates of the treasure chest.

(,   )

1 mark

④ Write the coordinates of the shark.

(,   )

1 mark

⑤ Write the coordinates of the pirate ship.

(,   )

1 mark

⑥ Translate the gold bar four squares to the left and six squares down.

1 mark

Graphs

There are many different graphs used to present data. These are the most common ones.

Pictograms

A pictogram is a way of showing information in a graph using pictures.

Items in a fruit salad:

Apple
Orange
Banana
Strawberry
Cherry
Pear

1 picture = 4 fruits

> **HINT**
> Always check the key to see what each picture presents.

① How many more strawberries than bananas were used?

1 mark

② How many items of fruit were used altogether?

1 mark

Bar Charts

A bar chart displays information by using rectangular bars of different heights. Along the bottom is information about the topic and there is a scale on the side.

> **HINT**
> Always look at the x- and y-axies carefully to understand the graph.

Height of children in maths club

Height in cm — Names of children

③ How many centimetres shorter is Susan than Katie?

1 mark

④ How tall are Ross and Mike in total?

1 mark

Answers on page 48

Line Graphs

A line graph is used to display information which changes over time. It is plotted on a graph as a series of points joined with straight lines.

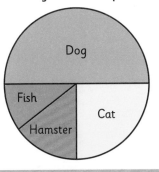

Average temperatures last week

HINT
Follow the gridlines from the x- or y-axis until your finger meets the line marked on the graph.

⑤ How many degrees did the average temperature drop from Monday to Tuesday?

1 mark

⑥ On which day was the average temperature 10°C?

1 mark

Pie Charts

A pie chart is a circular chart broken up into segments, or slices. Each segment represents a value. Understanding them relies on your knowledge of angles.

200 children were asked about their favourite pet:

HINT
Think back to your learning on fractions, percentages and degrees to help.

⑦ 10% said that fish were their favourite pets. How many children is that?

1 mark

⑧ 30 children named one pet as their favourite. Which pet was that?

1 mark

Parent Guide

Discuss with your child which style of graph they prefer. Why do they feel this is the best representation? Talk about which graph they find most tricky to interpret and the reasons why. Evaluating representation is an important way to become familiar with elements of graphs and how to approach them.

Answers on page 48

Answers

Page 4 - Addition and Subtraction

1 134 + 76 = **210**

2 2123 + 45 = **2168**

3 12356 + 34567 = **46923**

4 2456 + 3485 + 903 = **6844**

5 31.4 + 23.9 = **55.3**

6 31.23 + 0.87 = **32.1**

7 298.70 + 14.55 = **313.25**

8 314 − 203 = **111**

9 5609 − 4418 = **1191**

10 12318 − 309 = **12009**

11 38.9 − 27.6 = **11.3**

12 3498.70 − 23.65 = **3475.05**

13 9.00 − 3.18 = **5.82**

Page 5 - Addition and Subtraction Practice Questions

1 4897 + 67 = **4964**

2 9.2 + 121 = **130.2**

3 349 − 255 = **94**

4 392.6 − 63.2 = **329.4**

5 6.87 + 2.345 = **9.215**

6 8452 − 51 = **8401**

7 9 − 1.9 = **7.1**

8 27 + 121.8 = **148.8**

Page 6 - Multiplication and Division

1 245 × 3 = **735**

2 874 × 4 = **3496**

3 298 × 32 = **9536**

4 4309 × 26 = **112034**

5 210 ÷ 3 = **70**

6 567 ÷ 9 = **63**

7 480 ÷ 15 = **32**

8 1272 ÷ 24 = **53**

Page 7 - Multiplication and Division Practice Questions

1 412 × 7 = **2884**

2 9813 × 32 = **314016**

3 219 × 9 = **1971**

4 2112 ÷ 8 = **264**

5 814 ÷ 37 = **22**

6 123 × 6 = **738**

7 172 × 8 = **1376**

8 630 ÷ 18 = **35**

Page 8 - Order of Operations

1 20 − (4 × 2) = 12

2 (15 ÷ 5) − 3 = 0

3 23 − (18 ÷ 3) = 17

4 (3 × 2) + 6 = 12

5 17 + (3 × 6) = 35

6 (14 ÷ 2) − (10 ÷ 5) = 5

Page 9 - Order of Operations Practice Questions

1 45 ÷ ⟨20 − 5⟩ = **3**

2 35 ÷ ⟨5 × 7⟩ = **49**

3 ⟨9 × 3⟩ − 4 = 23

4 ⟨5 × 5⟩ − ⟨3 × 4⟩ = **13**

5 4 + ⟨7 × 5⟩ = **39**

6 20 − ⟨6 × 2⟩ = **8**

7 12 + ⟨3 × 2⟩ = **18**

8 50 − ⟨6 × 6⟩ = **14**

Page 10 - Place Value Calculations

1 57 × 10 = **570**

2 43.354 × 100 = **4335.4**

3 0.4 × 1000 = **400**

4 57 ÷ 10 = 5.7

5 43.3 ÷ 100 = **0.433**

6 4 ÷ 1000 = **0.004**

Page 11 - Place Value Calculations Practice Questions

1 76.23 × 10 = **762.3**

2 458 ÷ 1000 = **0.458**

3 8.2 ÷ 100 = **0.082**

4 0.9 ÷ 10 = **0.09**

5 5.1 × 100 = **510**

6 62.13 ÷ 100 = **0.6213**

7 62 ÷ 10 = **6.2**

8 22.2 × 1000 = **22200**

Page 12 - Percentage

1 25% = **28 + 28 + 14 = 70**

2 61% = **140 + 28 + 2.8 = 170.8**

Page 13 - Percentage Practice Questions

1 20% of 130 = **26**

2 25% of 460 = **115**

3 50% of 340 = **170**

4 51% × 300 = **153**

5 30% × 2000 = **600**

6 14% of 1600 = **224**

7 70% × 190 = **133**

8 11% × 567 = **62.37**

Page 14 - Adding and Subtracting Fractions

1 $\frac{2}{8} + \frac{3}{8} = \frac{5}{8}$

2 $\frac{7}{9} - \frac{2}{9} = \frac{5}{9}$

3 $\frac{4}{10} + \frac{5}{10} = \frac{9}{10}$

4 $\frac{5}{6} - \frac{1}{6} = \frac{4}{6}$

Page 15 - Adding and Subtracting Fractions Practice Questions

1. $\dfrac{4}{7} - \dfrac{3}{7} = \dfrac{1}{7}$
2. $\dfrac{1}{5} + \dfrac{3}{5} = \dfrac{4}{5}$
3. $\dfrac{5}{7} - \dfrac{1}{7} = \dfrac{4}{7}$
4. $\dfrac{2}{8} - \dfrac{1}{8} = \dfrac{1}{8}$
5. $\dfrac{2}{10} + \dfrac{1}{5} = \dfrac{4}{10}$
6. $\dfrac{11}{16} - \dfrac{2}{8} = \dfrac{7}{16}$
7. $\dfrac{1}{4} + \dfrac{2}{12} = \dfrac{5}{12}$
8. $\dfrac{4}{9} + \dfrac{1}{2} = \dfrac{17}{18}$

Page 16 - Multiplying and Dividing Fractions

1. $\dfrac{1}{3} \times 2 = \dfrac{2}{3}$
2. $\dfrac{3}{4} \times \dfrac{1}{2} = \dfrac{3}{8}$
3. $\dfrac{2}{5} \times 6 = \dfrac{12}{5}$
4. $\dfrac{4}{5} \times \dfrac{2}{3} = \dfrac{8}{15}$
4. $\dfrac{3}{4} \div 5 = \dfrac{3}{20}$
5. $\dfrac{1}{3} \div 3 = \dfrac{1}{9}$
7. $\dfrac{2}{5} \div 2 = \dfrac{2}{10}$
8. $\dfrac{3}{10} \div 4 = \dfrac{3}{40}$

Page 17 - Multiplying and Dividing Fractions Practice Questions

1. $\dfrac{1}{4} \div 3 = \dfrac{1}{12}$
2. $\dfrac{1}{2} \times 4 = \dfrac{4}{2}$
3. $\dfrac{2}{3} \times 9 = \dfrac{18}{3}$
4. $\dfrac{2}{4} \times \dfrac{4}{5} = \dfrac{8}{20}$
5. $\dfrac{4}{6} \times \dfrac{3}{9} = \dfrac{12}{54}$
6. $\dfrac{2}{3} \div 6 = \dfrac{2}{18}$
7. $\dfrac{2}{6} \times \dfrac{3}{4} = \dfrac{6}{24}$
8. $\dfrac{5}{7} \div 7 = \dfrac{5}{49}$

Page 18 - Place Value

1. Thirty-two million, four hundred and fifty-six thousand, one hundred and two.
2. Value of 1 = **100**
3. Value of 4 = **400,000**
4. **2**
5. **3** is in the ten millions column.
6. **32,456,103**
7. **32,456,002**
8. **0.336**
9. **0.226**
10. **6** is in the thousandths column.

Page 19 - Place Value Practice Questions

1. **£3,123,000   £1,500,000   £518,750   £280,000**
2. Three million, one hundred and twenty-three thousand.
3. **0.24m   1.23m   1.24m   10.4m**
4. 1 more: **3,942,310**   1000 more: **3,943,309**   100,000 more: **4,042,309**
5. **7** is in the tenths column.
6. 1 thousandth less: **0.751**

Page 20 - Negative Numbers

1. $3 - 6 = -3$
2. $-3 + 6 = 3$
3. $-1 - 3 = -4$
4. $-8 + 2 = -6$
5. **10**
6. **6**
7. **6**

Page 21 - Negative Numbers Practice Questions

1.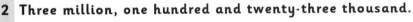
   -15 -14 -13 -12 -11 -10 -9 -8 -7 -6 -5 -4 -3 -2 -1 0 1 2 3 4 5 6 7 8 9 10 11 12 13 14 15
2. Floor 3
3. 5 metres
4. −3°C
5. 17°C
6. 22°C
7. 26 metres

Page 22 - Rounding

1. 5,000
2. 32,000
3. 7,800
4. 300,000
5. 460
6. $67 \times 4 = 70 \times 4 = $ **280**
7. $81 \times 5 = 80 \times 5 = $ **400**
8. $43 \times 6 = 40 \times 6 = $ **240**
9. $58 \times 3 = 60 \times 3 = $ **180**

Page 23 - Rounding Practice Questions

1. **33,000   32,600   30,000   32,620**
2. **£36.00**
3. **40×3**
4. **£4.00**
5. **453,000   452,700   450,000   500,000**
6. **5 metres**

Page 24 - Comparing Fractions

1 $1\frac{1}{4} = \frac{5}{4}$ **2** $2\frac{2}{3} = \frac{8}{3}$ **3** $3\frac{1}{2} = \frac{7}{2}$

Page 25 - Comparing Fractions Practice Questions

1 $\frac{2}{3} > \frac{3}{5}$ $\frac{2}{8} = \frac{1}{4}$ $\frac{2}{9} < \frac{1}{3}$ $\frac{3}{10} > \frac{1}{5}$

2 **Leigh** has eaten the most.

5
$2\frac{1}{4}$ — $\frac{11}{2}$
$5\frac{1}{2}$ — $\frac{15}{4}$
$3\frac{3}{4}$ — $\frac{9}{4}$

3 Ravi can make $5\frac{1}{2}$ quiches.

4 **Grace** has eaten the most of her apple.

6 $\frac{2}{4} = \frac{8}{16} = \frac{4}{8}$

Page 26 - Fractions, Decimals and Percentages

1 $\frac{13}{50} = \frac{26}{100}$ **2** $28\% = \frac{28}{100}$ **3** $0.14 = \frac{14}{100}$

4 $\frac{2}{10} = \frac{20}{100}$ **5** $0.02 = \frac{2}{100}$ **6** $3\% = \frac{3}{100}$

7 $0.3 = \frac{30}{100}$ **8** $32\% = \frac{32}{100}$ **9** $\frac{5}{20} = \frac{25}{100}$

Page 27 - Fractions, Decimals and Percentages Practice Questions

1 **Sinead** scored more.
4 **62%** of the ribbon is left.
6 Chin **studies** more.

2 **No, 13% of 25 is 52%**
5 **Ian** has gone the furthest.

3 5% $\frac{5}{10}$ 0.55

Page 28 - Ratio and Proportion

1 1:5 = 2:**10**
5 2:9 = 8:**36**

2 3:6 = 18:**36**
6 1:8 = 3:**24**

3 4:7 = 16:**28**
7 5:6 = **35**:42

Page 29 - Ratio and Proportion Practice Questions

1 $\frac{4}{9}$ black rabbits

6 16

2 3:2
4 **20** stones

3 4:5
5 24 shells

Page 30 - Units of Measurement

1 6 minutes
5 1140 seconds

2 3100 millilitres
6 2 days

3 49 days
7 36 months

4 4.2 kilometres
8 2000 metres

Page 31 - Units of Measurement Practice Questions

1 210 pages
4 3.6 kilometres
6 2 years

2 2400 millilitres

3 18 hours

5

Millimetres	Centimetres	Metres
150	15	0.15
2000	200	2
5000	500	5

Page 32 - 2D Shapes

1 4 sides, 4 vertices
5 **Regular** shape

2 3 sides, 3 vertices
6 **Irregular** shape

3 **Regular** shape

4 **Irregular** shape

Page 33 – 2D Shapes Practice Questions

Various answers are possible – examples:

1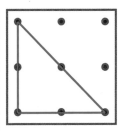

2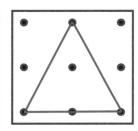

3

4 Radius = **5cm**

5 A3, B1, C4, D2

6 **A** and **F** are pentagons.

Page 34 – 3D Shapes

1 **5** faces, **9** edges, **6** vertices
4 **6** faces, **12** edges, **8** vertices
7 **Square-based Pyramid**

2 **3** faces, **2** edges, **0** vertices
5 **Cube**
8 **Cone**

3 **5** faces, **8** edges, **5** vertices
6 **Cuboid**

Page 35 – 3D Shapes Practice Questions

1

Number of faces	Number of edges	Number of vertices
5	**11**	**7**

4 **6** vertices

2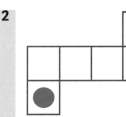

5 **3** faces

3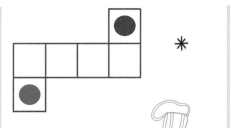

6 **12** straws

Page 36 – Perimeter, Area and Volume

1 Perimeter = **10cm**   **2** Area = **36cm²**   **3** Volume = **84cm³**

Page 37 – Perimeter, Area and Volume Practice Questions

Various answers are possible – example:

1

2 **11cm²**
5 **36 metres**

3 **24m²**
6 **1000cm³**

4 **£240**

Page 38 · Angles

1 **Acute** angle
4 70+50=**120**
180–**120**=**60°**

2 **Obtuse** angle
5 90+52=**142**
180–**142**=**38°**

3 **Right** angle
6 80+75+105=**260**
360–**260**=**100°**

Page 39 – Angles Practical Questions

1 Angle A = **90°**
4 Angle A = **130°**

2 Angle B = **106°**
5 Angle B = **50°**

3 Angle C = **37°**
6 Each angle = **60°**

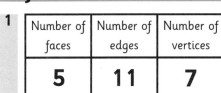
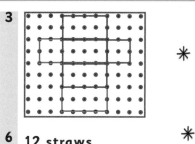

Page 40 - Coordinates

1 Yellow Square = (**-3,2**)
2 Blue Pentagon = (**-5,-2**)
3 Green Circle = (**1,-5**)

4
5
6

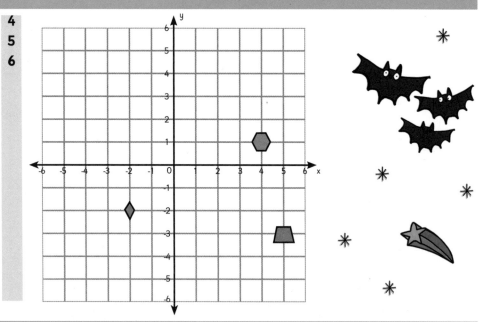

7

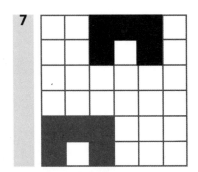

Page 41 - Coordinates Practice Questions

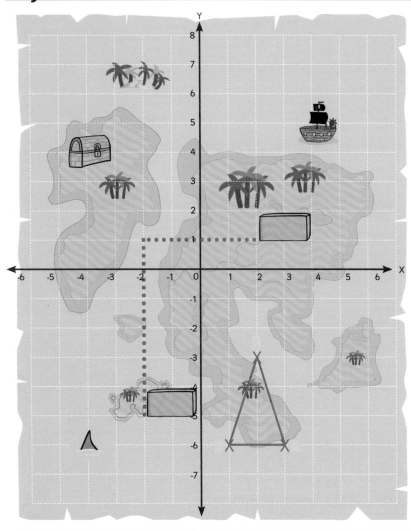

2 **Isosceles Triangle**
3 Treasure Chest = (**-4,4**)
4 Shark = (**-4,-6**)
5 Pirate ship = (**4,5**)

Page 42-43 - Graphs

1 22
5 4°C
2 84
6 Thursday
3 10cm
7 20
4 275cm
8 Hamster